NUMBER
TRACING

pre-k workbook

Published in the United States by Little, Brown Lab

Image Copyrights:
All images have been sourced from Shutterstock.com
Cover: Sasha Mosyagina
Interior: Sasha Mosyagina, oksanka00, Voronchihina Mariya, Helen Lane, Tim the Finn, Anastasia Boiko, Erica Truex, Pikovit, rangsan paidaen, Motorama, Alka5051, Skeleton Icon, Katja Gerasimova, Valenty, balabolka

Little, Brown Lab
Hachette Book Group
1290 Avenue of the Americas, New York, NY 10104
littlebrownlab.com

September 2018

Little, Brown Lab is an imprint of Little, Brown and Company, a division of Hachette Book Group
Little, Brown Lab name and logo are trademarks of Hachette Book Group, Inc.

ISBN 978-0-316-45588-6

www.littlebrownlab.com

LITTLE,
BROWN
LAB

NUMBER TRACING

pre-k workbook

For more fun pre-k and kindergarten workbooks, visit us at:

www.littlebrownlab.com

One funny dragon lives inside the forest.

one   one   one

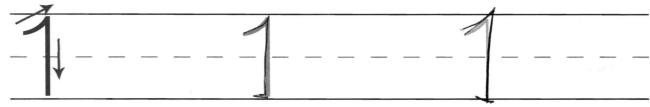

1   1   1

two   two   two

2   2   2

two   two   two

2   2   2

Two unicorns sleep beneath the stars.

two   two   two

2   2   2

three   three   three

3   3   3

three   three   three

3   3   3

Three pretty princesses have tea at the palace.

three three three

3 3 3

four   four   four

4   4   4

four   four   four

4   4   4

Four sailing boats are moving through the sea.

four four four

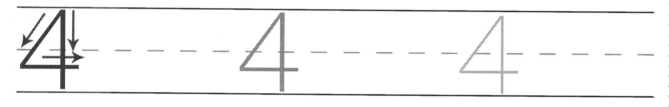

4   4   4

five   five   five

5   5   5

five   five   five

5   5   5

Five paper planes soar into the sky.

five   five   five

5   5   5

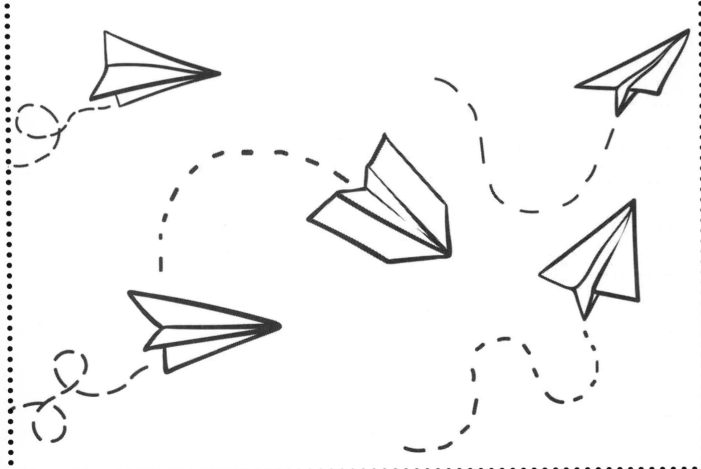

six   six   six

6   6   6

six   six   six

6   6   6

There are **six** cuddly kitties in the house.

six six six

6 6 6

seven seven seven

7   7   7

seven seven seven

7   7   7

Seven sea creatures swim beneath the ocean.

seven seven seven

7   7   7

eight eight eight

8 8 8

eight eight eight

8 8 8

Eight forest animals hunt for tasty acorns.

eight   eight   eight

8   8   8

nine   nine   nine

9   9   9

nine   nine   nine

9   9   9

In the garden, we smell **nine** beautiful flowers.

nine   nine   nine

9   9   9

ten   ten   ten

10   10   10

ten   ten   ten

10   10   10

Ten silly robots work at the big factory.

ten   ten   ten

10   10   10

one one one

1 1 1

one one one

1 1 1

On the road, there stands **one** giant castle.

one   one   one

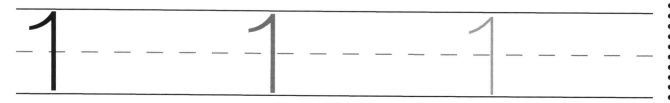

1   1   1

two   two   two

2   2   2

two   two   two

2   2   2

There are **two** brave knights on horseback.

two   two   two

2   2   2

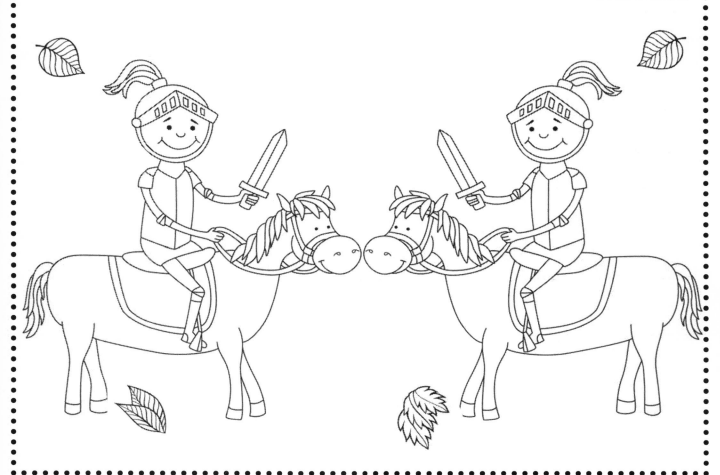

three   three   three

3   3   3

three   three   three

3   3   3

Under the sea, **three** beautiful mermaids swim.

three three three

3 3 3

four　four　four

4　4　4

four　four　four

4　4　4

Four little dolphins jump through the waves.

four four four

4 4 4

five   five   five

5   5   5

five   five   five

5   5   5

In the park, there are **five** playing puppies.

five   five   five

5   5   5

six six six

6 6 6

six six six

6 6 6

We can see signs for **six** tractors and trucks.

six six six

6 6 6

seven seven seven

7   7   7

seven seven seven

7   7   7

In the sky, we spy **seven** floating blimps.

seven seven seven

7   7   7

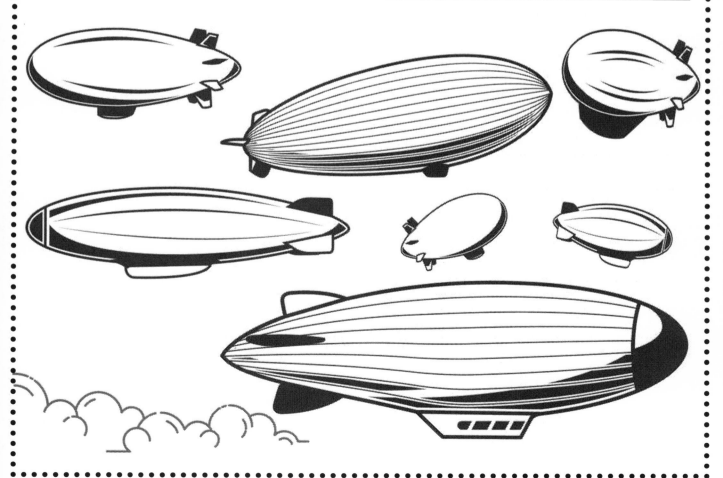

eight   eight   eight

8   8   8

eight   eight   eight

8   8   8

There are **eight** shiny cars parked in the garage.

eight   eight   eight

8   8   8

nine   nine   nine

9   9   9

nine   nine   nine

9   9   9

Through the telescope, we see **nine** distant planets.

nine   nine   nine

9   9   9

ten   ten   ten

10   10   10

ten   ten   ten

10   10   10

We race **ten** paper boats in the stream.

ten ten ten

10 10 10

Keep practicing!

Let's try 1-12!

one   one   one

1   1   1

two   two   two

2   2   2

three   three   three

3   3   3

four four four

4 4 4

five five five

5 5 5

six six six

6 6 6

seven seven seven

7　　　7　　　7

eight eight eight

8　　　8　　　8

nine nine nine

9　　　9　　　9

ten   ten   ten

10   10   10

eleven   eleven   eleven

11   11   11

twelve   twelve   twelve

12   12   12

one   one   one

1 - - - - - 1 - - - - - 1 - - - -

two - - - - two - - - two

2 - - - - 2 - - - - 2 - - - -

three - three - three

3 - - - - 3 - - - - 3 - - -

four   four   four

4   4   4

five   five   five

5   5   5

six   six   six

6   6   6

seven seven seven

7 ------- 7 ------- 7 -------

eight eight eight

8 ------- 8 ------- 8 -------

nine nine nine

9 ------- 9 ------- 9 -------

ten   ten   ten

10   10   10

eleven eleven eleven

11   11   11

twelve twelve twelve

12   12   12

one   one   one

1   1   1

two   two   two

2   2   2

three   three   three

3   3   3

four   four   four

4   4   4

five   five   five

5   5   5

six   six   six

6   6   6

seven seven seven

7 7 7

eight eight eight

8 8 8

nine nine nine

9 9 9

ten ten ten

10 10 10

eleven eleven eleven

11 11 11

twelve twelve twelve

12 12 12